THE EASY PLANT-BASED DIET

CLEAN AND HEALTHY EATING TO LOSE WEIGHT & ENERGIZE YOUR BODY. | INCLUDE SHOPPING LIST.

PAMELA KENDRICK

CONTENTS

Introduction   v

Benefits Of A Plant Based Diet   1

SHOPPING LIST

SHOP FOR:
1. Bread, Rolls, and Pasta   17
2. Dairy   18

CHECK YOUR PANTRY FOR:
1. Oils, Vinegar & Condiments   21
2. Flavoring   22
3. Nuts, Seeds, & Fruits   24
4. Dry Goods   26
5. Refrigerator Items   27

Conclusion   29

Copyright ©, 2021 by Pamela Kendrick.

No part of this publication may be reproduced or transmitted in any form or by any means, mechanical or electronic, including photocopying or recording, or by any information

storage and retrieval system, or transmitted by

email without permission in writing

from the author.

Neither the author nor the publisher assumes any responsibility

for errors, omissions, or contrary interpretations of the

subject matter herein. Any perceived slight of any

individual or organization is

purely unintentional.

INTRODUCTION

On a journey to discover other alternatives to traditional diets, registered dietitians often depend on cookbooks to help make the transition smooth. Healthy eating can mean different things to many people. It doesn't have a direct or simple definition. However, we have been able to use Plant-based Diet Cookbook for Beginners to teach and inspire readers to incorporate healthy eating practices into their lives. With an emphasis on beginners, this book perfectly captures some of the healthiest ways to eat.

Plant-based diets come in many stripes; though diet plans that entirely omit meat get the most attention, they're relatively uncommon. Most vegetarians eat a Lacto-ovo diet, which contains fruits and veggies, soy, beans, nuts, and grains, and some animal byproducts like eggs, dairy, and honey. However, vegans do not eat animal products, and beegans eat honey. The pescatarian diet is everything like the Lacto-ovo vegetarian diet, but with the addition of fish. Some new addition includes the flexitarian diet, a form of Semi-vegetarianism that eats massive plants and light animal products, and Mediterranean diet that is considered one of the healthiest ways of eating because they feed heavily on plants. But there are growing evidence that plant-based

Introduction

diets are linked with health benefits such as lower blood pressure, cholesterol, blood sugar, and reduction in body weight. This healthy lifestyle often results in less risk of diabetes, cancer, health disease, and other diseases. Eating a plant-based diet will lower the risk of health conditions and help you live longer.

One of the most impactful steps you can take to improve your health, increase energy levels, and prevent chronic diseases is to change your diet to a plant-based diet. Over the last decade, science has shown that changing your nutrition is one of the most important ways to live longer, help the environment, and reduce your risk of getting sick. However, you've always heard of a plant-based diet, and you are probably thinking that moving to a plant-based diet sounds like a good idea, but you have no idea how and where to get started. Don't worry, you bought the right book, and I firmly believe you are in the right place. We've used our tools, expertise, and insight to develop a comprehensive plant-based cookbook to make your change plant-based diet easy and enjoyable. This book will answer most of your questions; provide you with helpful advice on some of your favorite plant-based recipes that you need.

Unlike other cookbooks, this cookbook is designed for beginners. It makes extensive use of simple terms to help beginners and non-beginners relate to the plant-based recipe's complexities. The idea is to remove the general intricacies associated with plant-based diets. So that you can easily choose a dish from the array of available options, dive in, and prepare it. This cookbook doesn't contain only plant-based recipes. It also gives detailed information on calories, nutrition, healthy eating pattern, food rules, and the best time to consume a diet. The recipes are full of colorful, nutrient-rich vegetables and fruits and other affordable diets.

The whole book is a useful plant-based recipe combination for beginners who are making a conscious effort to change their food philosophy and approach to a plant-based recipe on a low budget. The recipes section is organized into three categories: Breakfast, lunch, and dinner. Also, this categorization includes Salads, Snacks, Desserts, and Smoothies. Each recipe is designed to

Introduction

provide the right serving guide and includes some nutrient information. You'll find recipes from different cuisines in this cookbook. Since we are more focused on beginners, we did an excellent job by including colorful images at the beginning of each chapter and topic by giving a pictorial description of what to do and how to do them.

Although the book is for beginners, it is also perfect for plant-based eaters who want to add more healthy recipes to their original plant-based diet or who have lost the momentum of eating plant-based food. This book presents a great way to introduce you to or get back to a majority plant-based eating lifestyle. The book describes what it means to feed on a plant-based diet and go on to teach you about the nutrients of each diet and the health implication of eating a plant-based diet.

This plant-based cookbook is full of gut-healthy, anti-inflammatory recipes, along with great information on meal prep and nutrition. Every recipe in this book is carefully selected to meet your needs. The book is narrative and contains easy-to-understand nutrition information. Being flexible with your diet is an essential aspect of healthy eating, and I think Plant-based Diet Cookbook for Beginners highlights that aspect perfectly.

A full nutritional analysis of each recipe is included, and the recipe instructions are written in a short ingredient list to make readers feel comfortable, not intimidated.

It's hard to say which recipe is my favorite However, I will leave you to pick yours. I wish you a great time and good health as you create magical diets using the recipes from this cookbook.

BENEFITS OF A PLANT BASED DIET

- A plant-based diet will help lower your blood sugar.
  - A plant-based Diet May Keep Your Heart Healthy
  - A plant-based diet may prevent type 2 diabetes.
  - A plant-based Diet Could Help You Lose Weight
  - A plant-based diet is rich in Omega-3 Fatty acids.
  - A plant-based diet will help you live longer.
  - A plant-based diet is rich in zinc.
  - A plant-based diet may decrease the risk of cancer.
  - A plant-based diet improves cholesterol.
  - A plant-based diet is rich in iron.
  - A plant-based diet minimizes your risk of stroke.
  - The plant diet keeps your brain strong.
  - A plant-based diet may help with calcium connection.
  - A plant-based diet may help to reduce inflammation.
  - A plant-based diet serves as a healthy alternative to animal vitamin B12
  - A plant-based diet helps maintain a healthy weight.
  - A plant-based diet makes you look younger.
  - A plant-based diet may help lower blood pressure
  - A plant-based diet protects the environment.

- A plant-based diet prevents diseases.
- A plant-based diet stabilizes blood sugar.
- A plant-based diet is economical.
- A plant-based diet is rich in protein and vitamins
- A plant-based diet regulates digestion.
- A plant-based diet is good for the skin and hair.
- A plant-based diet can help fight seasonal sickness.
- A plant-based diet is rich in protein.

☐ A plant-based diet will help lower your blood sugar.

According to the Physicians Committee for Responsible Medicine , a plant-based diet can make a difference in your health. Health complications such as high blood pressure or hypertension may expose you to other health challenges such as heart disease, stroke, and type 2 diabetes. However, several studies have shown positive results that a plant-based diet can reduce blood pressure, thereby lowering your blood sugar. A 2014 meta-analysis JAMA Internal Medicine explored data from 39 studies. It concluded that individuals who feed on plant and animal products (omnivorous diets) have higher blood pressure than people who feed on plant-diets only. In addition, vegetarians had a thirty-four percent lower risk of developing hypertension than nonvegetarians.

☐ A Plant-Based Diet May Keep Your Heart Healthy.

An average vegetarian has much lower cholesterol level than a meat-eater. This is because plant based-diets are usually low in saturated fats and contain little or no cholesterol. Animal products are high in saturated fats, which is dangerous to your health when consumed excessively. Since cholesterol is found in animal products such as dairy, meat, and eggs, reducing your animal products or meat consumption means you are less likely to suffer from a heart problem. According to the Journal of the American Heart Association published in August 2019, eating a plant-based diet may reduce your risk of developing cardiovascular disease by sixteen percent and the possibility of dying from the complicated cardiovascular disease by about thirty-one percent. Besides, the type of protein in a plant-based diet helps in reducing cholesterol. Many studies show that replacing animal protein with plant protein will lower blood cholesterol levels. This perhaps is another important advantage of a plant-based diet. But eating healthy isn't about limiting your meat consumption alone; you have to make sure you consume a plant-based diet in the right proportion. This means your diet has to contain legumes, whole grains, fruits, olive oil, and other plant product in the right proportion. Even if the amount of meat and fat product in your diet stays the same, adding plant-based food to your diet could be a game-changer to helping you achieve a healthy heart. According to the 2018 review published in the journal Progress in Cardiovascular Diseases , eating a plant-based diet can also help reverse coronary health disease and reduce CHD's risk by forty percent. In addition, a plant-based diet may reduce the risk of hypertension, which is a risk factor for heart disease. These studies show that a plant-based diet has a clear advantage over others. Considering the fact that heart-related diseases are the most fatal killer in America, plant-based diet ability to significantly lower heart disease risk is a huge win.

☐ **A plant-based diet may prevent type 2 diabetes.**

There's a strong connection between what you eat and type 2 diabetes. Weight is a major risk factor when it comes to type 2 diabetes. Plant-based diets are high in complex carbohydrates and fiber and these are the best dietary prescription for controlling diabetes. Fatty tissues make the body cell more resistant to insulin and increase the damaging effect of this disease. To avoid this disease, medical practitioners have recommended a plant-based diet. Consuming a plant-based diet filled with high-quality plant foods reduced the risk of developing type 2 diabetes. This is because plant-based diets are lower in saturated fats than animal-based diets. This is why a vegetarian has a lower chance of developing type 2 diabetes. Vegetarians were 74 percent less likely to develop diabetes over 17 years compared to those who ate meat at least once per week. Because a plant-based diet is high in fiber and plant compounds with antioxidant activities that can help regulate blood sugar, they are also useful in managing existing diabetes. A diet based on legumes, vegetables, whole grains, and fruits is extremely low in fat and sugar and can lower blood sugar levels or reduce the patient's need for medication. Since patients with diabetes have a high risk of heart-related diseases, avoiding a diet that contains fat and cholesterol is essential, and a plant-based diet is the best way to achieve this.

☐ **Plant-Based Diet Could Help You Lose Weight.**

Eating a plant-based diet can help you drop pounds. Some people claim some food diet could help you lose weight in the short run, only to gain every pound back the moment you stop it. Plant eaters tend to weigh less even when losing weight isn't the primary reason for consuming plant-based food. Your chances of suffering from obesity decrease when you switch from an animal-based diet to a plant-based one. The primary reason for changing your diet to a plant-based diet might be because you want to eat healthy by nourishing the body and cells to maintain good health, but weight loss can be a by-product of replacing and reducing certain foods. There is a sustainable body mass index (BMI) between a plant-based eater and a meat product eater. That means, if the BMI for a plant-based eater is 23.6, the BMI for a meat-based eater can be as high as 28.8, which qualifies as overweight. Plant-based diet help to lose weight because whole grains and vegetables are low on the glycemic index, which means they digest slowly. In addition, the antioxidants and fiber in fruits help to prolong fullness. Plant-based diets offer a functional take on a healthier lifestyle, which means the steps you take forward in your health are more realistic and achievable with less stress. If weight loss is your goal, then It's incredibly important to prioritize and feed on a healthy, quality plant-based diet.

☐ **A plant-based diet is rich in Omega-3 Fatty acids.**

Omega-3 may be helpful to pregnant women and people with chronic health conditions. A good source of plant-based omega-3 acid includes ground flaxseeds and flaxseed oil, chia seeds, and organic canola oil. Although the plant-based omega-3 doesn't easily convert to EPA and DHA, they are healthy and good for growth.

☐ **A plant-based diet will help you live longer.**

If all the potential benefits of eating a plant-based diet could be summarized into two major words, it will be "live longer." According to The Journal of the American Heart Association , a plant-based diet lowers the risk of all causes of mortality by 25 percent. It increases your immunity from most forms of diseases. When you build your diet from a generous array of vegetables, grains, beans, and fruits, living a healthy life becomes remarkably easy. When you consume a plant-based diet, you will experience a major improvement in your cholesterol, blood sugar, heart function, and many other health aspects. All these factors come together to make you live longer. It's pretty simple to cut down on food that is high in fat and increase plant product consumption will make you experience good health and long life.

☐ **A plant-based diet is rich in zinc.**

Plant-based diets are a good source of zinc. Zinc is essential for wound covering, blood sugar control, and the immune system. Plant food such as whole grain, tempeh, beans, lentils, nuts, and seeds are a good zinc source. However, phytates compounds in plant foods may hinder the body from absorbing zinc; you can improve this by soaking the plant food in water for hours before cooking.

☐ **A plant-based diet may decrease the risk of cancer.**

This is yet another good reason to opt for a plant-based dinner tonight. A plant-based diet has numerous health benefits, and one of such benefit is that it helps reduce the risk of cancer. The American Institute for Cancer Research claims a diet rich in vegetables, fruit, grains, beans, nuts, seeds, and some animal foods contain protective nutrients, such as fiber, vitamins, minerals, and phytochemicals that can help decrease the risk of cancer. Vegetarians have a significantly lower rate of colon cancer than meat-eaters, and colon cancer has been closely linked with meat consumption than all other dietary factors. A review published in

2011 in Cancer Management and Research states that the protective benefits present in plant-based foods such as fiber, vitamins, and minerals could lower the risk for certain cancers by about 10 percent. The plants-based diet contains a cancer-fighting substance called phytochemicals, and vegetarians consume a lot of vegetables, which contains plant pigments called beta carotene and lycopene . This substance may explain why plant-based eaters have less lung and prostate cancer. Besides, research has shown that a diet that contains fewer meat products and contains more plant products may reduce prostate and ovarian cancer risk to a large extent. A 2012 meta-analysis in the Annals of Nutrition and Metabolism claims that plant-based eaters have an eighteen percent lower risk of cancer than non-vegetarians. This is a result of the plant diet's immune-boosting properties. These immune-boosting properties do not only decrease the risk of cancers, but they also promote a healthy weight.

☐ **A plant-based diet improves cholesterol.**

Bad cholesterol LDL is damaging to the body; it may lead to fatty deposits in the blood, restrict blood flow, and cause stroke, heart attack, and other related heart diseases. However, according to a review of 27 studies published by The American Journal of Cardiology, consuming a strictly plant-based diet can help reduce cholesterol levels by twenty-five percent. While combining animal products with plant-based diet can lower bad cholesterol by ten to fifteen percent. In addition to decreasing bad cholesterol, a plant-based diet also decreased HDL (good) cholesterol but in a much smaller proportion to bad cholesterol LDL. However, some of these researches have failed to explain why vegetarians have more natural killer cells that can identify and destroy cancer cells.

☐ **A plant-based diet is rich in protein.**

Proteins are made up of amino acids used to build and repair muscle, skin, bone, and the immune system. The body also needs protein to make hormones and enzymes. Although the body can make amino acids, the body cannot make essential amino acids, hence consuming rich plant-based diets such as beans, peas, nuts, soy products, vegetables, and whole grains.

☐ **A plant-based diet is rich in iron.**

Iron is the mineral in the blood that carries oxygen. Therefore, getting a sufficient amount of iron is essential for everyone. Plant food such as whole grain, cereals, dark green vegetables, fruits, seeds, dried beans, and peas are fortified with iron. Irons in a plant-based diet is healthier, although they are not easily absorbed in the body like those found in animal products. In addition, eating an iron-rich plant diet and vitamin C helps your body make better use of iron.

☐ **A plant-based diet minimizes your risk of stroke.**

If you already have high blood pressure, overweight, diabetes or heart disease, high cholesterol, and you smoke, drink, or use drugs, you are potentially at the risk of stroke. However, most of these risk factors can be minimized if you consume more of a plant-based diet and decide to live a healthy lifestyle. One of the first steps to take in this direction is to increase your consumption of fruits and vegetables. You decrease your risk of developing stroke by twenty-one percent when your diet contains a higher percentage of fruits and vegetables.

☐ **The plant diet keeps your brain strong.**

The physiological benefits of following a plant-based diet are many, but there are some possible mental ones, too. Eating an extra 100 grams of fruits and vegetables per day (about one-half cup) will lead to a thirteen to fifteen percent reduction in the risk of cognitive impairment and dementia. This is because the cornerstones of a plant-based diet, which are fruits, vegetables, and whole grains, are rich in polyphenols. Polyphenols may help slow the progression of Alzheimer's disease and may help reverse cognitive deterioration. A meta-analysis in the journal Frontier in Aging Neuroscience claims that an increase in the consumption of fruits and vegetables can lead to a twenty percent reduction in the risk of cognitive impairment and dementia. This is likely due to the antioxidants in plants that clean up cellular waste (free radicals) and protect cells from damage. In addition, plant-based diets can improve your memory largely by preventing the degeneration of the mind. It is believed that body stress and inflammation lead to generative diseases and neurodegeneration. Therefore, it is important to consume a plant-based diet to help minimize these diseases.

☐ **A plant-based diet may help with calcium connection.**

Excessive consumption of animal protein may lead to loss of calcium from the bone. Therefore, you need to replace animal products with a plant-based diet to reduce the amount of calcium lost. Besides, vegetarians are less likely to form kidney stones or gallstones, and because they eat little or no animal product, they are also at a lower risk for osteoporosis. This explains why plant-based eater have little osteoporosis, even when their calcium intake is below daily consumption.

☐ **A plant-based diet may help to reduce inflammation.**

Inflammation is caused by a series of health issues such as heart disease, cancer, chronic inflammatory diseases. However, a plant-based diet rich in vegetable, fruit, and whole wheat has plenty of carotenoids, flavonoids, and phytonutrients, also known as plant chemicals. Help eliminate free radicals capable of damaging the DNA, prompt inflammatory response, strengthen the immune system, and reduce inflammation.

☐ **A plant-based diet serves as a healthy alternative to animal vitamin B12.**

The body needs vitamin B12 for nerve functions and also for the production of the red blood cell. The lack of vitamin B12 can lead to abnormal or damaged nerve functions and anemia. Most B12 comes from animal products, but this essential vitamin can also be sourced from a rich plant-based diet.

☐ **A plant-based diet helps maintain a healthy weight.**

The ups and downs that come with traditional dieting can be stressful. But, if you seek to maintain a healthy weight without dieting, then you should consider cutting down on meat and embracing a plant-based diet. Plant-based diets are naturally rich in fiber, which increases satiety. When you consume a strictly plant-based diet, it's easier to maintain a healthy weight. A plant-based diet makes it easier to lose weight without counting calories. People who consume a plant-based diet have a lower obesity rate, heart disease, diabetes, and lower body mass (BMI) than those who eat meat. In addition, people who consume plant-based diets tend to be leaners than those who consume meat diet. Changing an eating habit is the cornerstone of maintaining and achieving a healthy weight permanently.

☐ **A plant-based diet makes you look younger.**

A plant-based diet promotes healthy cellular aging. According to the American Journal of Epidemiology study conducted in 2018, a diet rich in fruits, vegetables, whole grains, low sugar, salt, and processed meats contains a nutrient that slows down aging. Besides, a plant-based diet also prevents chronic health conditions that become more common as we age.

☐ **A plant-based diet may help lower blood pressure.**

An increasing number of studies show that vegetarians have a lower blood pressure than non-vegetarians. Meat is high in sodium, and when consumed excessively, it can significantly raise blood pressure level. When a patient with high blood pressure begins to consume a plant-based diet, many are able to eliminate the need for medication.

☐ **A plant-based diet protects the environment.**

Consuming a plant-based diet not only benefits people's health but also protects the environment. Plant-based diet help to maintain a healthy environment by creating smaller environmental footprints. A plant-based diet reduces greenhouse gas emissions, water consumption, and factory pollution. This sustainable diet can heal the world and reduce contribution to global warming and environmental degradation. According to the research published by The American Journal of Clinical Nutrition , A major contributor to climate change in the United States is the means by which we cut down on animal products and support a plant-based diet. The US food production system uses eighty percent of freshwater, fifty percent of total land area, and seventy percent of the fossil energy used in the country. And with a projected increase in population, the food production system is likely to take more of these resources. By not eating meat or reducing the amount of meat product in your diet in favor of plants, the earth's impact and carbon footprint will lessen. In addition, if you can take your plant-based diet "in-house" and grow your plants, you are helping to cut down on this impact and be more sustainable.

☐ **A plant-based diet prevents diseases.**

Eating plant-based whole food can slow down, prevent, halt, or even reverse chronic or minor diseases and keep you healthy. Plant-based diets may help people prevent or manage diabetes, heart disease, coronary heart disease, and type 2 diabetes by improving insulin sensitivity and reducing insulin resistance.

☐ **A plant-based diet stabilizes blood sugar.**

Research and medical journal have shown that plant diet improves blood glucose levels in patients suffering from diabetics or may potentially suffer from it in the future. Therefore, the consumption of a plant-based diet can lower the risk of diabetes-related medical conditions and reduce reliance on medications.

☐ **A plant-based diet is economical.**

A plant-based diet is relatively cheap and available than the animal product. In general, a plant-based diet cost lower than animal food, and they are healthy. When you switch to a plant-based diet, you will save more money at the supermarket and save more time in the kitchen while staying healthy. Best of all, a plant-based diet can be a tasty and enjoyable way to eat.

☐ **A plant-based diet is rich in protein and vitamins.**

Hemp seeds can be consumed raw, cooked, or roasted. They are also a great source of protein, vitamin E, and minerals.

☐ **A plant-based diet regulates digestion.**

Plant-based diets are packed with antioxidants, which are beneficial for people dealing with constipation, and they also help the digestive system and boost daily energy.

☐ **A plant-based diet is good for the skin and hair.**

A plant-based diet promotes cell growth and repair dry and damaged skin.

☐ **A plant-based diet can help fight seasonal sickness.**

Although plant-based diets are known to prevent and reduce the damaging effect of chronic and long-term disease, a plant-based diet can also keep you from getting the common cold or the flu each year. Consuming more of a plant-based diet will help your body defend its immune system and reduce the risk of disease. Fruits, vegetables, legumes, nuts, and seeds and forgoes animal products are rich in antioxidants that can strengthen your immune system and fend off seasonal illnesses such as the flu.

SHOPPING LIST

This list outlines everything you need to make all the recipes, plus the soups, desserts, salads, snacks, appetizers with drinks and smoothies.

SHOP FOR:

- Chopped fresh baby spinach
  - Potatoes
  - Artichoke hearts
  - Celery
  - Lettuce
  - Agave raw
  - Baby greens
  - Brussels sprouts
  - Cherry & Sun-dried tomatoes
  - Zucchini
  - Collard leaves
  - Courgette
  - Organic rose petals
  - Fresh sage
  - Bay leaves
  - Mushrooms
  - Fresh baby kale
  - Bell peppers (mixed colors)
  - Carrots
  - Basil leaves

- Radishes
- Fresh rosemary
- Mozzarella
- Golden cauliflower
- Arugula
- Asparagus spears
- Cucumber
- Radish
- Cabbage, red
- Sweet potato

1
BREAD, ROLLS, AND PASTA

- Corn tortillas
  - Breadcrumbs
  - Rotini
  - Whole grain bread
  - Hamburger buns
  - Ditalini pasta
  - Whole wheat linguine
  - Puff pastry
  - Elbow pasta
  - Whole-grain rustic bread
  - Whole grain sandwich wraps
  - Tortilla wraps
  - truRoots Organic Fusilli Pasta
  - Whole foods organic ziti

2
DAIRY

- Cotija cheese
    - Ricotta cheese, full-fat
    - Vegan cream cheese (Tofuti brand)
    - Cheddar cheese
    - Mozzarella cheese
    - Feta cheese
    - Ricotta cheese, full-fat
    - Vegan cream cheese (Tofuti brand)
    - Cheddar cheese
    - Mozzarella cheese
    - Feta cheese

CHECK YOUR PANTRY FOR:

1
OILS, VINEGAR & CONDIMENTS

- Maple syrup
  - Honey
  - Avocado or peanut oil
  - Pancake cereal
  - Extra virgin olive oil spray
  - Black currant syrup
  - Olive oil
  - Rice vinegar
  - Peanut butter
  - Apple cider vinegar
  - Balsamic vinegar
  - Vegan butter
  - Canola oil
  - Coconut oil
  - Unsalted butter
  - Agave syrup
  - Coconut cream
  - Almond butter

2
FLAVORING

- Grounded turmeric
    - Onion (yellow, purple, green & red)
    - Sea salt
    - Jalapeño
    - Grounded coriander
    - Grounded cumin
    - Dried thyme & dill
    - Salt (black & white)
    - White rum
    - Currants
    - Cayenne
    - Smoked Paprika
    - Tahini
    - Marjoram
    - Kombucha
    - Grounded rosemary
    - Red curry paste
    - Sriracha
    - Taco seasoning
    - Grounded nutmeg

Shopping List

- Italian seasoning
- Brown sugar
- Tomato paste
- Tamari
- Cinnamon sugar
- Kosher salt
- Chili flakes
- Grounded pepper
- Grounded cinnamon

3
NUTS, SEEDS, & FRUITS

- Firm tofu
  - Chia seeds
  - Mango
  - Lime
  - Millets
  - Pineapple chunks
  - Sunflower seeds
  - Corn grits
  - Quinoa
  - Pistachios
  - Cardamom
  - Couscous
  - Peaches
  - Almonds
  - White Rice
  - Garbanzo beans
  - Lentils
  - Nutmeg
  - Kiwi
  - Strawberries

Shopping List

- Medjool dates
- Cacao nibs
- Cranberries
- Tart cherries
- White quinoa
- Butternut squash
- Chickpeas
- Peanuts
- Pine nuts
- White beans
- Pomegranate seeds
- Papaya
- Brown rice
- Pitted dates
- Pumpkin
- Ripe bananas
- Pecans
- Flax seeds
- Corn kernels
- Walnuts
- Cashew
- Lemon zest
- Black beans
- Avocado

4
DRY GOODS

- Garlic powder
  - Nutritional yeast
  - Cornstarch
  - Rolled oats
  - Curry powder
  - Arrowroot powder
  - Chili powder
  - Almond powder
  - Oat flour
  - Cornstarch
  - Chickpea flour
  - Cocoa powder
  - Baking powder
  - Dry bread crumbs
  - Pectin powdered
  - Whole wheat flour

5

REFRIGERATOR ITEMS

- Unsweetened almond milk
  - Soy milk
  - Guacamole
  - Soy & Apple sauce
  - Frozen blueberries
  - Tequila
  - Fresh parmesan
  - Seltzer
  - Mushroom broth
  - Frozen mango
  - Stir-fry sauce
  - Frozen raspberries
  - 1/2 cup of basil pesto hummus
  - Pineapple juice
  - Marinara sauce
  - Ice cubes
  - Arrabbiata or tomato sauce
  - Frozen peas
  - Salsa
  - Soy milk & Eggs

- Buffalo wing sauce
- Cornmeal
- Vegetable broth
- Light beer
- Plain Greek yogurt,
- Harissa sauce
- White wine
- Dark chocolate chips
- Espresso shots
- Lime juice
- Hot dog buns
- Whole milk
- Pumpkin puree
- Vanilla extract

CONCLUSION

Generally, we all agree that you will likely gain more benefits from cutting down on meats and animal products, which contains higher saturated fat and calories. But when it comes to eating healthy, it goes beyond what you don't eat or what you limit. What you eat and add to your diet is more important. The desire to live a healthy life and find a better substitute for basic diet is fundamental to good health, hence consuming more plant-based products. Consuming more of Plant-based is about staying healthy by eating more vitamins, minerals, fiber, and phytochemicals, which are the nutritional component that is usually in low quantity in our basic diets.

Whether you're a committed plant-based diet eater or just curious about this increasingly popular diet, which has so many health and environmental benefits. This cookbook contains some of the most intrinsic recipes that will take you on a mouth-watering journey while converting to a plant-based diet. This book is fortified with delicious everyday plant-based recipes, as well as nutritional information, calories, practical advice on how and when to change your diet. A lot of helpful tips about stocking your kitchen; the best way to follow recipes, shopping

Conclusion

economically for plant-based foods and food prep suggestions. This book goes beyond the average plant-based cookbook that is generally packed with inspirational ideas for incorporating more vegetables into your diet.

From juices and smoothies that range from the Frozen Mojito to the indulgent Pina colada in a pineapple; too quick and creative ideas for breakfast, such as Tofu Scramble, Banana Oats Pancakes, Egg Spinach Muffins, Papaya Boat Parfait, and Ginger Marmalade. The hearty and filling lunch and dinner, including variations on much-loved staples like Tortilla Veggie Pizza, Portobello Fajita, Hummus Collard Wraps, Grilled Street Corn, Vegan Creamy Pasta with Kale, Vegan Mushroom Bean Burger, Broccoli Tofu Stir-Fry, Vegan Pumpkin Risotto, and Eggplant Parmesan. Our favorite soup and snacks such as Potato Leek Soup, Mediterranean Cabbage Soup, Lentil Soup, Cherry Pie Energy Balls, and Sweet Potato Nachos are also included in this cookbook to give it an all-embracing outlook. This book dissipates all traditional claims that plant-based diets are too restrictive or difficult to follow.

The book is super fun, approachable, and has so many creative recipes. It is filled with delicious and easy recipes backed by science-based nutrition information. In addition, the book also extensively discusses the advantages of a plant-based diet, covers issues that result from inflammation in a very approachable way, and delivers recipes that work every single time. On most pages, you'll not only get a recipe but a research snippet on why the food is a good choice.

The choice to switch over to a plant-based diet or not is a personal decision. The choice is often associated with our upbringing, values, identity, and relationship with animals. However, the choice to make sure your transition is smooth and easy is up to us. If you had also tried plant-based recipes before and ditched it because you feel it is boring or cumbersome, this book is a collection of creative, delicious, and fun recipes to help you make the most from your plant-based diet.

Meeting your daily nutritional need with Plant-based Diet

Conclusion

Cookbook for Beginners has never been made easier. Grains, beans, and vegetables are rich in protein and iron. Green leafy vegetables, lentils, tofu, nuts, and banana oat are excellent calcium sources. Vitamin D is a naturally occurring vitamin; it is normally made in the body when the sun shines on the skin. However, if your body has difficulty producing vitamin D, you can easily obtain it from fortified or commercial foods such as cereal, soymilk, multivitamin, and other supplement products. Pregnant and woman breastfeeding mothers need to get enough vitamin B12 (cyanocobalamin), a good source includes common vitamins gotten from vegetables, mushrooms pumpkins and broccoli. All these are the benefit you will gain from this cookbook.

This cookbook is meant to give you an idea of how to fix a plant-based diet and to give you a wide variety of recipes that you can use to create magic. Yes, I know you want to live a healthy life; you wouldn't be reading this book if you don't. I encourage you to follow the plate method step-by-step with helpful descriptions of diets and visuals for making a balanced plant-based diet, as shown in this book, to achieve the healthy lifestyle you desire.

www.ingramcontent.com/pod-product-compliance
Lightning Source LLC
Chambersburg PA
CBHW071550080526
44588CB00011B/1850